No Flag Large Enough

NO FLAG
LARGE ENOUGH

Frances Crowe's 2018-2019 collected columns
from the
Daily Hampshire Gazette

Haley's

Athol, Massachusetts

Copy edited by Mary-Ann DeVita Palmieri.
Graphics editing by Mark Wright.

Haley's
488 South Main Street
Athol, MA 01331
haley.antique@verizon.net

Library of Congress Cataloging-in-Publication Data
Names: Crowe, Frances, 1919- author.
Title: No flag large enough : Frances Crowe's 2018-2019 collected columns
from the Daily Hampshire gazette / Frances Crowe.
Other titles: Daily Hampshire gazette.
Description: Athol, Massachusetts : Haley's, [2020] | Summary: "No Flag Large Enough compiles the columns written during her ninety-ninth and hundredth years by the Northampton, Massachusetts activist Frances Crowe. A longtme resister of war, nuclear weapons, and nuclear power, Frances Crowe influenced many in the Massachusetts Pioneer Valley and beyond"--Provided by publisher.
Identifiers: LCCN 2020005910 (print) | LCCN 2020005911 (ebook) | ISBN
9781948380317 (paperback) | ISBN 9781948380324 (ebook)
Subjects: LCSH: Pacifism--United States. | Political participa-tion--United States. | Peace movements--United States. | United States--Politics and government.
Classification: LCC JZ5584.U6 C76 2020 (print) | LCC JZ5584. U6 (ebook) | DDC 303.6/60973--dc23
LC record available at https://lccn.loc.gov/2020005910
LC ebook record available at https://lccn.loc.gov/2020005911

For Frances,
who changed our lives

There is no flag large enough to cover the shame of killing innocent people.

—Howard Zinn

Contents

Issues, Actions, and Community: Read On
a foreword by Caltha Crowe, Frances's daughter xiii

Visiting Frances at Home 1
an introduction by Dave Eisenstadter
editor, *Valley Advocate*
features editor, *Daily Hampshire Gazette*

Radical Activism 5

The First Time I Was Arrested. 9

No One Wins a War 15

Hitchhikers and the Path to Peace 19

Anthrax and Me 23

Films That Change People's Minds. 27

My One-Hundredth Birthday Wishes. 31

How Can We Work Together?. 35

What Can We Do, Today, About Climate Change? 39

In It Together 43

I Couldn't Imagine No *Democracy Now!*. 47

Nuclear Freeze. 51

Resisting Nuclear Submarines. 55

Learning That War Is Not the Answer 59

Photos

Frances celebrates her hundredth birthday . . . . frontispiece

Frances climbs a fence to risk arrest 11

Peggy Seeger's album cover features Frances 12

Frances joyfully risks arrest at Vermont Yankee 33

Amy Goodman interviews Frances at Smith College 48

Frances's peace buttons decorate an Asian robe 63

Frances's light shines on 65

Issues, Actions, and Community: Read On

a foreword by Caltha Crowe, Frances's daughter

Whenever my late mother was asked, "How many times have you been arrested?" she would respond without missing a beat, "Not enough." Her one-hundred-year-and-six-month life journey was a remarkable one, traveling from small-town, conservative Missouri to a life of finding her radical soul.

My mother, Frances Hyde, was born on March 15, 1919, in Carthage, Missouri, a small town close to the Mason-Dixon line where the Civil War had never completely ended, at least in people's hearts and minds. Jim Crow ruled the town, the Ku Klux Klan was in ascendance during her childhood, and Frances recalled a public hanging. The Hyde family were Catholic, and in the early 1920s, many in southern Missouri considered Catholics a dangerous force. Frances remembered a childhood friend telling her that the Catholic church basement was full of bombs and guns in preparation for a planned uprising against the rest of the town. Social class ruled small-town Carthage in all interactions. As Frances helped her mother run wet laundry items through a crank-style wringer, her mother, Anna, told her, "Frances, Carthage is not the place for you."

Frances listened to her mother and moved out of Carthage physically, socially, and mentally. By the time Frances reached her mid thirties, she was a Quaker, a peace and environmental activist, and a person who had committed her life to creating a better world. The transformation began early for Frances. She campaigned for physical education for girls in her elementary school. She and her friend Ginny Williams began the International Club in Carthage—as far as I know a club of two ten-year-old girls who got together on Saturday mornings to make fudge and write letters promoting world peace.

A person with strong intellectual drives, Frances attended and graduated from Syracuse University. Despite her father's adamant objections, her mother supported the effort, supplying money saved from selling eggs laid by her back-yard chickens for the train ticket to Syracuse. During World War II, Frances took classes at Mount Holyoke College, Columbia University, and the New School for Social Research. A passionate reader, Frances read steadily throughout the busy years of raising her children and until the last weeks of her life. It was impossible to have a conversation with Frances that did not include, "Have you read . . . ?" She was always ready to discuss, analyze, and go deep with her current reading. Persistent and courageous, Frances was unstoppable when she took on an issue. When one of her sons was born deaf, our parents visited schools for the deaf all over the country to find the right one. Frances learned to be a teacher of the deaf in order to teach her son to speak, not a popular approach to deaf education in the early 1950s. When she learned that testing atomic bombs in the atmosphere poisoned her children's milk, she launched a massive petition drive to stop atmospheric bomb testing.

Such qualities served her as, driven by a vision of a better world, she immersed herself in opposition to the Vietnam War by establishing a draft resistance and counseling center in our family's basement. Her involvement in the campaign against nuclear weapons led her to witness against such weapons in a deeply person way. She canoed out to nuclear submarines off the Connecticut coast to pour vials of her own blood on the vessels. Work against apartheid, her active support for the rights of refugees from Central America, demonstrations to shut down the local nuclear power plant, and countless other actions led to her multiple stints in jails and prisons, one lasting thirty days. Local sheriffs came out to meet her when they saw her long arrest record. When Frances received an award from the Ralph Nader foundation, Mr. Nader commented, "She embodies persistence."

The scope of the change she worked to create was broad. As she said, "Let us work together to build a new society with health care, tuition-free education through graduate school, and healthy food for all. Let us build a new society in the shell of the old." Growing most of her food in her front yard, walking everywhere she went for as long as she could, speaking out at every opportunity, and supporting progressive media, Frances embodied the lifestyle she endorsed.

Frances walked the walk.

Frances was an appreciator. Every year on my birthday, I received a written message relating Frances's thoughts on my positive qualities. From her deathbed, Frances called as many people as possible, including her four-year-old great grandson, to tell them how they had positively affected her life.

We never know the effect we have on other people. After Frances's death, letters poured in from all over the country. Many mentioned her courage and commitment to a better world. All mentioned her kindness.

The book you are about to read is compiled from a series of columns Frances wrote for her hometown newspaper, Northampton's *Daily Hampshire Gazette*. She wrote the first when she was ninety-nine years old and the last six months after her hundredth birthday.

As was always true of Frances, the columns are not about her but rather about issues, actions, and community that she shared actions with.

Read on.

*Frances Crowe and some of her family in Northampton celebrate her
one hundredth birthday, March 15, 2019.
Among family, from left, front: Frances; her great-grandson, Vincent (Vinny) Dinelli;
Vinny's mother, Frances's granddaughter, Rosa Frances Crowe-Allison Dinelli with
her son, Frances's great grandson, Vito Dinelli;
Simone Crowe, Frances's granddaughter; Louis Dinelli, Rosa's husband;
from left, back, Nancy Crowe, Tom Crowe's wife and Frances's daughter-in-law, and
next to Nancy, Frances's niece Sara Murray*

Visiting Frances at Home
an introduction by Dave Eisenstadter
editor, *Valley Advocate* • features editor, *Daily Hampshire Gazette*

What was to be my final interaction with Frances Crowe was unannounced. As her editor, I had a couple of questions about one of the columns contained here, and my deadline approached. As usual for me, I didn't have any luck trying to reach her by phone or email, so I tried calling on her at home. Being at her home was a thing of wonder—from the multitude of activist lawn signs in her front yard to the giant portraits of inspirational women and large stacks of books in her living room.

When I arrived that day in August 2019, the door hung open in the breeze, and she called from her kitchen for me to come on in. For someone so knowledgeable about hate and violence in the world, she had great trust in fellow people. And she was sharp as a tack, even at a hundred years old. Out of her vast library, she knew the exact book to consult to find the answer to my question and the name of the person referenced who would answer it. I checked the spelling of his name with her, and she gave a different spelling than listed in the book. When I looked it up later, she had the correct spelling. The book was wrong.

You likely don't need me to tell you that Frances Crowe is an activist institution in the Valley and well beyond. And that's why, even though she lived a full life to age one hundred, the community still deeply feels her passing. Her dogged commitment to stopping war, ending nuclear power and nuclear weapons, and protecting the environment has been, and continues to be, a vital part of Northampton's history and a source of inspiration for all of us.

It wasn't long after I first joined the staff of the *Daily Hampshire Gazette* in late 2014 that I found myself writing about Crowe —she would receive an honorary degree from Smith College the following year—and eventually interviewing her in her home. Over the past years, as I became editor of the *Valley Advocate* and the Gazette's *Hampshire Life* magazine, Crowe has come up again and again for her continued work. Just a month before her death, we had her on the *Advocate's* cover—an old photo of police leading her away with arms held behind her back and a smile on her face. Behind her, *Advocate* art director Jennifer Levesque placed a large nuclear symbol, representing one of her biggest lifelong fights against nuclear weapons and nuclear energy. Next to Crowe were the words *Seventy-four years since Hiroshima and Nagasaki: Local antinuclear activists speak.*

That's far from the only time the *Advocate* has featured Crowe. Even in my short tenure with the paper, I remember another feature we did in part on her called *Radical Moms: Using the power of motherhood to make political change.* At the time, Crowe told reporter Chris Goudreau that she didn't pay federal taxes. "I file and I send the money to the Iraqi Children's Art Exchange that will go to the cancer hospital in Baghdad. I send the money to the victims of war," she said.

Crowe's columns—which she wrote for *Hampshire Life*—are nothing short of revelatory. In one of the last ones she wrote, she detailed how in the 1980s she carried a baby bottle full of her own blood to dump onto a newly commissioned nuclear submarine—a parody of the popular practice of smashing a champagne bottle on the prow of a new ship. And she succeeded. She found the injuries she received from the crowd "worth it," she said, including having her hair pulled and her face and arms scratched—she was doing her part to protest the proliferation of nuclear weapons.

Getting arrested was part of life for Frances Crowe, and she said she couldn't count the times she was arrested. But here's how she characterized the amount to the *Daily Hampshire Gazette*: "Not enough." Truly, how much more inspirational does it get?

The collected columns give us insight into Crowe's lifelong activism and her passion about causes she supported. And while she is no longer among us in the physical realm, her words constitute a fitting complement to other aspects of her legacy, including the now-closed Vermont Yankee nuclear plant she railed against for decades and the daily broadcasts— which she orchestrated—of the progressive radio show *Democracy Now!*

Radical Activism
September 2018

As I reflect on nearly a century of community interaction, involvement with humanitarian agencies, radical activism, and commitment to the Quaker way, I contemplate my roots in a thriving Missouri town, Carthage.

1919, the year I was born, ushered in a decade of prosperity and optimism at the end of "the war to end all wars." My mother took me to my first march when the soldiers from Carthage came home. I was only a baby, but I have always had the feeling that war has defined my life.

My three sisters and I grew up in a solid Midwestern family, and our parents stressed the importance of social awareness. In keeping with prevalent custom, my spirited, active mother stayed home while my father ran his prosperous plumbing and heating business. Looking back on our upbringing in an observant Roman Catholic home, I realize the influence of our household on the commitments of my later life.

Tom Crowe, my late husband, and I moved to Northampton in the middle of the twentieth century after his time in the military and mine in the defense industry during World War II. A practicing radiologist, Tom knew full well the devastating implications of atomic and hydrogen bombs. When we, the United States, dropped atomic bombs to kill tens of thousands of civilians in Hiroshima and Nagasaki at the end of the war, I knew instantly that I had to devote my life to resisting nuclear weapons. Soon, I would realize that I had to resist nuclear power. And I always knew that I had to resist war.

Tom and I shared a deep concern that we had opened Pandora's box by splitting the atom to develop nuclear weapons. I knew I could not be silent, and I knew that we would find a way to make a difference. In the early years of our marriage, we concentrated on finding work for Tom and raising a family. Early on, with one of our three children deaf, we investigated ways to support the unique individual personalities of our three children. After much consideration, Tom bought a medical practice in 1951 in Northampton that allowed us to be near the Clark School for the Deaf.

In Northampton, we also found supportive activist communities and Quaker meeting. Eventually, in coordination with the Society of Friends, I founded a branch of the American Friends Service Committee. We encouraged civil rights, countered apartheid, supported migrant workers, resisted nuclear weapons, and opposed nuclear power plants. As the years passed, AFSC offered a platform for opposing war in Vietnam, the Middle East, and elsewhere in the world. Through AFSC, I provided draft counseling about conscientious objection, especially to the war in Vietnam, to some two thousand young people.

I affiliated myself with national and international peace action groups, including the Women's International League for Peace and Freedom. In the early 1960s, Gertrude "Trudy" Huntington and I founded the Jane Addams WILPF branch in Northampton with more than 125 members.

When the situation warranted, I sometimes crossed the line to do civil disobedience. I spent time in jail.

With the opportunity to write a regular column for *Hampshire Life*, I hope to review moments from my long life of witnessing for peace and justice.

In many ways, those moments began back in Carthage, Missouri. As the second of four sisters, I saw my older sister as a model child always doing what our parents told her, rarely stepping out of line. I decided that I had to do things differently if I were going to be noticed.

Our parents did not discourage my bid for individuality.

My first significant action occurred when I was in high school in the 1930s. I worked to have physical education classes for girls and joined others in standing up to oppose the Junior Reserve Officers Training Corps.

Something had stirred in me to oppose war.

That something lives and breathes in me to this day.

The First Time I Was Arrested
October 2018

By the time my husband, Dr. Thomas Crowe, and I moved to Northampton in the 1950s, we had decided to oppose war after the US dropped bombs on Hiroshima and Nagasaki at the end of World War II. Eventually, I became director of the American Friends Service Committee of Western Massachusetts, headquartered in Northampton.

By 1955, the United States had embroiled itself in a war in Vietnam, Cambodia, and Laos. The Vietnam War Wall in Washington, DC, memorializes 58,220 American lives lost during the war, which ended in defeat for the US in 1973.

We rarely memorialize the more than 4.3 million Vietnamese civilians, soldiers, and Viet Cong fighters who died during the Vietnam War. We often fail to mention the more than 275,000 Cambodians and 20,000 to 62,000 Laotians who died during the Vietnam War as the result of internationally illegal bombing of Cambodia and Laos.

American opposition to the Vietnam War began to boil in the late 1960s when I counseled some 2,000 potential US soldiers in their applications for status as conscientious objectors. With the dawning of the 1970s, Cleo Gorman of Northampton and I organized a group called Women Against the War.

We decided to stage a peaceful demonstration at Westover Air Force Base in Chicopee on March 8, 1972, International

Women's Day. Terrifying photos of civilian Vietnamese casualties had increasingly emerged since 1968. We protested at Westover because the Air Force trained B52 bomber crews there for eventual bombing duty in Vietnam, Cambodia, and Laos.

Some thirty of us dressed in black pajamas, traditional garb of rural Vietnamese women. We hoped bystanders would feel the suffering of Vietnamese women if we dressed like them. We also hoped that young men facing conscription or drafting into the US military would see the humanity of the Vietnamese people and examine their consciences about entering the army. At the time, the US had not determined that women were eligible for combat.

We proceeded to Westover's gates where a line of Air Force airmen stood between us and the base entrance.

We didn't intend to risk arrest. We brought Vietnamese poetry to read. As we read it aloud, we found ourselves moved to tears. We conferred among ourselves and blocked the entrance. The airmen arrested us. We hoped that our radical action would encourage other Americans to oppose the war in Vietnam, Laos, and Cambodia.

The judge at our trial sentenced me to community service, and I arranged to make a presentation about nonviolence at a local elementary school. I hoped that the children would understand that we can solve differences without resorting to violence.

We'll never know for sure if our actions on International Women's Day in 1972 influenced any Westover personnel or bystanders to oppose the war or refuse to be part of the US military. For many years, as part of my work with AFSC, I had counseled young men on how to become conscientious objectors. You never know what may cause someone to turn his back on war.

According to the law, anyone conscientiously opposed to participation in war on moral or ethical grounds with the same degree of intention as religious grounds qualifies for designation as a conscientious objector.

Though I was one woman working out of a home office in the basement, I had a copy of the law and the help of Bill Norris, a dedicated lawyer. We wanted to help those listening to their conscience and saying, "War is not the answer."

Let us work together to build a new society with health care, tuition-free education through graduate school, and healthy food for all. Let us build a new society in the shell of the old.

photo by Nancy Clover

Frances climbs the fence at
Seneca Falls Army Depot in 1988 to protest Cruise missiles.

PEACEFUL WOMAN, FIGHTING HARD

Peggy Seeger sings five peace songs in honour of Frances Crowe of Northampton, MA

Peggy Seeger's album cover features soldiers taking Frances into custody at Seneca Falls Army Depot in 1988.

No One Wins a War
November 2018

No one wins a war, including one waged by an all-volunteer military as employed and deployed by the United States today.

Pacifists and realists warned us against the ill-advised invasion of Afghanistan seventeen years ago when we began the war there in the wake of attacks on the Pentagon and World Trade Center. Our unresolved interventions in Central America, South America, and the Persian Gulf, Iraq, and Syria perpetuate devastation, displacement, rape, pillage, and a heartrending, widespread refugee challenge that divides public opinion and, by itself, threatens world peace.

US military spending amounts to fifty-four percent of the federal budget, according to National Priorities Project. The US military budget exceeds the *combined* military budgets of the next seven highest military spenders in the world: China, Saudi Arabia, Russia, United Kingdom, India, France, and Japan, in order of their expenditures. In a vicious circle, Saudi Arabia, the UK, and Japan buy much of their military hardware from us.

In any war, arms traders prosper along with their investors in the face of sacrifices by taxpayers, those targeted by war, and those trained by the United States to constant combat readiness. Despite attractive prospects advanced by military recruiters, men and women who volunteer and deploy to fight our wars rarely find promised rewards without strings attached.

Suicide, post traumatic stress, homelessness, readjustment issues, and employment challenges meet returning veterans. A June, 2018, US Veterans Administration report cites 20.6 military or veteran suicides every day, 16.8 daily by veterans and 3.8 daily by active-duty personnel, amounting to 6,132 veterans and 1,387 service members who die annually by suicide. At least 10 percent of deployed veterans return with PTSD, according to the VA.

Some 30 percent of veterans returned with PTSD from our war in Vietnam, where the US accepted defeat after some two decades of war that took almost 60,000 US lives and millions of Southeast Asian lives. We fought the Vietnam War with conscripted or drafted soldiers, all men at the time, as well as those who enlisted in all branches of the military.

The Selective Service System supervised the draft, and US towns and cities each had a group of citizens, the draft board, to select and induct young men for military training. The military then taught inductees to use weapons and kill before assigning them to war-related duties.

I knew I had to act when our teenaged son Tom and some of his classmates from Williston Academy stood around our kitchen unsure that they wanted to be conscientious objectors. That marked a turning point for me. I knew I had to raise awareness about the evil of war.

I decided to act on my profound belief that morality prohibits war and killing. I had studied psychology and advertising during my college and post graduate years, and I recognized subliminal persuasions about patriotism, heroism, and service that encouraged support for the US military.

I wanted to confront the distortions and encourage young men to search their consciences and recognize their own reluctance to kill. I wanted them to realize that the military exists to kill, and I wanted to assist them in filing for status as conscientious objectors in the face of the draft. The government would assign some COs to alternative service, and some COs would be exempted from service.

In order to begin my work, I took a workshop about conscientious objection for a weekend with the Central Committee for Conscientious Objectors (CCCO) in Philadelphia and another about group process at the University of Massachusetts.

By 1967, soon after we moved into our smaller house in Northampton, I was ready to embark on my quest to assist young men in announcing to their draft boards and to US society that "War is not the answer."

Hitchhikers and the Path to Peace
December 2018

"There is no flag large enough to cover the shame of killing innocent people," reads a poster hanging on a wall in my home. Howard Zinn wrote the words in his 1986 essay, "Terrorism over Tripoli."

As a Quaker, a member of the Society of Friends, I oppose war and take every opportunity to exercise the moral obligation to encourage resistance to war, weapons, and political actions that foster war.

President Trump recently sent some 5,800 US military troops to create a human wall along our border with Mexico to keep Central American immigrants from entering our country. Fifty years ago, in 1968, President Richard M. Nixon commanded approximately 545,000 US troops in Vietnam.

While all of the troops now along the US southern border volunteered for the military, just about a quarter of Vietnam-era soldiers had been drafted into the United States Army through the United States Selective Service System.

In 1968, I decided I wanted to oppose the draft by encouraging young men to search their consciences and apply for conscientious objection according to US law.

Young men then qualified as draftees to military service because, identified as 1-A, they met physical and mental requirements for induction into the US Army. I wanted young men to resist the draft by qualifying as 1-0, called conscientious objectors. To qualify as 1-0, each man had to demonstrate his moral opposition to war and killing. Each 1-0 would reduce a local draft board's quota by one man.

After preparing myself by attending seminars on conscientious objection and group process, I decided to invite young men to come to me for draft counseling in the basement office in my home. At first, in the days before social media, I placed an ad in a conventional newspaper.

It didn't work.

Then, I wrote a personal letter to area clergy and lawyers asking for their help. No one responded at first, but late in that week, Bill Norris, a lawyer from Cummington, agreed to help me with pro bono legal advice.

Encouraged, I got into the family station wagon the following Monday morning to drive between Northampton and Amherst in order to pick up hitchhiking draft-age men. In those days when no buses ran along Route 9, many hitchhikers sought a lift, and I had no qualms about picking them up. I handed my riders a mimeographed flyer urging them to attend a session in my home about legal alternatives to the draft if they opposed the war.

I learned that many of them planned to avoid the draft by resettling in Canada or Sweden. Even worse, some entertained cutting off the tip of an index finger to be declared 4-F, unfit for induction into the army according to the selective service system.

The next day, my basement filled with young men looking for a moral, legal alternative to becoming part of the US military. I had questionnaires for them from the Valley Peace Center, and soon a vibrant draft counseling operation began. It went on for more than six years.

I orchestrated the sessions on Tuesday and Thursday afternoons and Friday evenings. I encouraged the young men to search their consciences for moral concerns that demonstrated their opposition to killing. We worked at finding ethical reservations that would convince a draft board to grant 1-0 status regardless of religious belief. We applied the question of John Woolman, nineteenth century abolitionist and Quaker preacher, "What are you objecting to?"

Soon, young men helped facilitate, and they helped each other enormously. Their experience became invaluable with filing applications and facing draft boards. Pioneer Valley students encountered draft boards all over the country, and we learned effective approaches.

Depending on circumstances, a 1-0 classification led to alternative service in a hospital or government agency. Sometimes a 1-0 classification meant an exemption from service of any kind.

In all, according to the citation accompanying my 2015 honorary doctorate from Smith College, I counseled more than two thousand young men during the Vietnam-era draft.

War is not the answer.

Anthrax and Me
January 2019

Only when individuals start saying no to immorality will the world become a better place. When a person acts in conscience, it changes not only the world for the better but also the person.

Students from UMass came to me in 1989 to discuss Pentagon-funded studies of anthrax on the UMass campus. The students had searched their consciences and decided that the UMass anthrax studies were immoral.

We met in the American Friends Service Committee office in my Northampton home to discern how the students, AFSC, and I might resist the UMass anthrax studies.

The students felt that the late Curtis Blaine Thorne, professor of microbiology, had undertaken research in order to weaponize anthrax. The federal Center for Disease Control identifies anthrax as a dangerous agent likely to be used in bioterrorism. "*Bacillus anthracis*, the bacteria that causes anthrax, would be one of the biological agents most likely to be used," according to the CDC. "Biological agents are germs that can sicken or kill people, livestock, or crops."

The international community banned the use of chemical and biological weapons after World War I and reinforced the ban in 1972 and 1993 by prohibiting the development, production, stockpiling, and transfer of such weapons, according to the International Committee of the Red Cross.

It didn't take long for the students and other Pioneer Valley residents to act. The May 31, 1989, *New York Times* reports

> Even for the Amherst campus, where protests are not exactly rare, the events of this spring have been unusual. The demonstrators, attacking not only the Pentagon research but also, to a lesser degree, what they see as societal racism and sexism, have taken over campus buildings at least four times this month, held a weeklong hunger strike, and staged a mock wedding between the university and the US Defense Department. There have been 154 trespassing arrests. Some students have been taken into custody two or three times, and several sympathetic townspeople who occupied the university chancellor's office were also seized.

In order to support the 1989 protests at UMass, I asked the lawyer Cristobal Bonifaz to read and provide us with a copy of Dr. Thorne's contract with the Pentagon. The contract was, of course, a matter of public record between a federal agency and the university. Dr. Thorne insisted that his studies involved potential enemy use of anthrax and said, therefore, that his studies supported defense. After reading the contract, Mr. Bonifaz supported the conclusion that Dr. Thorne worked on weaponized anthrax on behalf of the US government. MIT's Dr. Jonathan King, founder of Science for the People, agreed with Mr. Bonifaz in support of the students.

Many students who acted in conscience at UMass in the 1980s against weaponized anthrax had participated in Dr. Terisa Turner's seminar concentrating on Marxist political and social theories.

Although townspeople asked the Amherst Board of Health to outlaw anthrax research on the UMass campus in the late 1980s and early 1990s, the board of health refused on grounds that there was no danger to townspeople. The UMass faculty senate voted to support Dr. Thorne's research in the name of academic freedom.

Nevertheless, protests against Dr. Thorne's studies continued. Eventually, while never acknowledging that he worked on weaponized anthrax, Dr. Thorne gave up Pentagon funding for his work.

In 2014, Dr. Sigrid Schmeltzer of the UMass history faculty invited me to participate in Dr. King's Science for the People program. Recently, Dr. Turner visited me and gave me a copy of the book *Takeover*, which she edited with Timothy A. Belknap. A collection of documents relating to the 1980s and 1990s protests at UMass, *Takeover* was published by the International Working Group, Inc.

Students, residents of the Pioneer Valley, and I acted in conscience during protests against 1980s and 1990s Pentagon-funded studies of anthrax at UMass. Eventually, Dr. Thorne gave up the funding, and surely each of us who acted grew in our understanding of conscience and morality.

During recent weeks, I have been inspired by young women taking leadership of protests against US gun violence and at the climate change summit in Poland.

Films That Change People's Minds
February 2019

"Not to know is bad," goes an African proverb. "Not to wish to know," it continues, "is worse."

My sentiments exactly.

When we have real information and not fake news, we often find motivation to act in keeping with conscience. Over the many years, I have found that film (now often called video) makes a wonderful catalyst for providing information and stimulating discussion.

Whether sponsored by Northampton Committee to Stop the Wars, Sut Jhally's Media Education Foundation, or American Friends Service Committee, film moves people to act.

Almost fifty years ago, as our government continually misled people about what really went on in Vietnam, I decided to show *The Quiet Mutiny*, the first of sixty documentary films by the prolific Australian documentarian John Pilger. During the Vietnam war years, he won British press association awards for excellence in journalism as he drove out the truth about the Vietnam war.

People in our area didn't know much about what was really going on in Vietnam in the 1960s and 1970s. As part of my AFSC activities, I showed *The Quiet Mutiny* to a full house in my basement and then orchestrated a discussion. We all found it enlightening and shocking, and many people grew committed to ending the war. Over time, I showed many documentary films.

In those days before YouTube, the internet, and Netflix, I had to operate a 16-millimeter sound projector after driving a considerable distance to pick up the film roll in a heavy metal 20x20x2-inch can. Sometimes during a showing, a film broke, and I'd have to repair it with Scotch tape.

Eventually, always to illuminate people's understanding and often in cooperation with Forbes Library, the resistance community, or Mount Toby Society of Friends, I showed movies about apartheid in South Africa, injustices in the Middle East, lack of ethics and greed of weapons manufacturers, potential horrors of impending wars in Central America, Iraq, Afghanistan, and more.

Encouraging discussion after showing films always brought light to issues and issues to light as the film and conversation moved us to resistance action.

Slowly, technology evolved from film cannisters through VHS tapes and DVDs to current possibilities of streaming movies directly through a laptop to a computerized projector.

For different causes, I've found especially effective films. We showed *Gods of Metal* to question the use of nuclear weapons, *When the Mountains Trembled* about El Salvador, Guatamala, and Romero, and *Controlling Interest, the World of the Global Corporations*. David Goodman's *Witness to War* provides a clear ethical message.

In 1991, Sut Jhally, professor of communication at UMass, Amherst, founded Media Education Foundation, located for a long time on Masonic Street in Northampton. We showed films every week there for fourteen years in cooperation with MEF until Woodstar Café expanded into the space. We always had a good discussion.

Since 2004, Northampton Committee to Stop the Wars has sponsored frequent films about peace and justice for discussion, often showing as many as one a week. Find a list of all films shown at northamptoncommittee.org/films/. Carolyn Toll Oppenheim often coordinates Northampton Committee showings.

One of my favorite stories about a film dates back to when I had to drive somewhere to pick up a film canister. My friend Johnnetta Cole, who later served as president of Spelman College and director of the Smithsonian Institution's Museum of African Art, taught with the UMass anthropology faculty. She played a key role in founding the UMass department of African-American Studies.

Johnetta called me one day after she left UMass to suggest I show *Last Grave at Dimbaza* and orchestrate a discussion to encourage universities and individuals to stop investing in South African countries because of apartheid.

I arranged to get the movie, scheduled to arrive in time to show it to UMass trustees at lunch during one of their meetings. After a hair-raising runaround, I picked up the film cannister and arrived at UMass just in time to show the movie to the trustees. Riveted, they watched it during lunch and barely touched their chicken salad.

Trustees eventually voted to divest from South Africa in the late 1980s.

Film and discussion have powerful potential to change minds and win hearts and souls to right action.

My One-Hundredth Birthday Wishes
March 2019

Since my birth a hundred years ago in Carthage, Missouri, many things have changed.

Sadly and unconscionably, the capacity of the United States to wage war, exploit the Third World, contribute to climate disruption, and marginalize the poor has changed only for the worse.

Biplanes carrying World War I flying aces morphed into nuclear bombers after the so-called "war to end all wars"— which, it didn't. When I was twenty-six, the United States fulfilled its demonic dream of harnessing nuclear energy for weaponry, dropped atomic bombs to destroy the Japanese cities of Hiroshima and Nagasaki, and opened Pandora's Box to the potential devastation of not only nuclear weapons but also nuclear power.

When I was growing up in Carthage, such horror never occurred to us.

United States imperialism marches unchecked and immoral throughout the world, these days without welcoming refugees whose homes we've destroyed. Once we had the longest unguarded border in the world, and once the Statue of Liberty proudly welcomed " . . . tired, . . . poor, . . . huddled masses yearning to breathe free"—the ancestors of all of us.

In the deceitful name of regime change or democratization, we've devastated Iraq, Afghanistan, Central American nations, and Syria just as, before I was born, the United States fostered the genocide of Native Americans, South Pacific islanders, and others.

Unchecked United States industrialism and our addiction to automobiles, airplane travel, and industrial food, to name a few, have contributed to the greatest climate crisis since the great Ice Age. The rich get richer and the poor get poorer. It's a barbarous old story.

Television hadn't been invented when I grew up in Carthage, never mind computers. We didn't know anything about digitization or streaming. We had telephones, and a human being, usually a woman, personally asked for the number we wanted when we picked up our handpiece to initiate a call: "Number, please?" We might find ourselves listening in to other calls on what we called a party line.

My father, William Chauncey Hyde, ran a heating and plumbing business, and we had the most modern furnace and indoor plumbing. Like everyone else in those days before electric or gas refrigeration, we had an icebox on our porch. The iceman came every few days with refill blocks of ice so that our food would stay cold.

Women got the right to vote the year I was born. We had a Ford motor car with running boards—six-inch-wide, rubber-covered metal strips that ran the length of the car. Some of the boys loved to stand on them. Maximum speed? Sixty-five miles per hour, although likely without boys standing on the running board.

We had a Victrola to play hard rubber records in the days before vinyl. RCA Victor Corporation trademarked the name Victrola, and ten-inch grooved disks often played on only one side. We cranked the Victrola so that the disk revolved on a turntable. Then we moved a metal arm down to the turning disk so that the arm's needle reverberated through a mechanical speaker to reproduce the sounds in the disk's grooves.

Frances joyfully risks arrest as she did tens of times at Vermont Yankee Nuclear Power Plant, which closed in 2014. Dorthee (her full name) and Ellen Graves, to right from Frances, help hold a banner that says Shut Down Vermont Yankee.

Most women wore dresses, and I do not remember women who wore slacks when I was a child. My mother, Anna Heidlage Hyde, made our clothes. My mother worked hard in our home with the help of an African American woman who came once a week to assist with cleaning. Carthage at least once sponsored a public hanging, which my mother thought was deplorable.

One of my older woman cousins studied physical education, and I admired her independence. I loved physical games, and I certainly remember the days when women's basketball meant that each team remained on just one half of the court.

Since my birth a hundred years ago, the United States has legalized contraception and abortion, passed sweeping civil rights laws, and integrated public establishments, including schools.

As I prepare to celebrate my hundredth birthday on March 15, I hope that the United States and its citizens find the moral insight and courage to stop war of all kinds, end the exploitation of other countries and our own citizens, begin to stop climate disruption by eating local and driving less, end the use of nuclear weapons and nuclear power, and foster fair and equitable employment for all workers.

What a happy birthday it would be if all my wishes came true.

How Can We Work Together?
April 2019

Over the years, I've learned that community action, the kind that can change the world, begins with the simplest question once two or more people have established their commitment to changing immoral or otherwise hurtful corporate, government, or community policies.

"How can we work together?" begins the conversation that can transform everything.

When a community begins to organize, participants do not necessarily know how positive transformation will occur nor when nor where. They may undertake detailed courses of action and make specific plans, but they also know that the ways of true transformation mean belief in possibility and good outcomes, some of them unanticipated.

Although our world still knows tragic war and the consequences of war, including nuclear weapons and nuclear power, I have experienced and witnessed many successful efforts of community organization leading to transformation and good outcome.

Through vigorous and effective community action, we

- brought *Democracy Now,* Amy Goodman's wonderful television and radio program, to central Massachusetts and established our own community radio station
- saw a freeze that lasted for years on US production of nuclear weapons, although the threat now grows

- witnessed the closing of the Vermont Yankee Nuclear Power Plant
- participated in ongoing weekly vigils to oppose United States war mongering and United States sanctions against other nations
- confronted defense industries, including General Dynamics, Raytheon, GTE, Bath Iron Works, and Lockheed-Martin in civil resistance actions that involved jail time for some participants
- resisted University of Massachusetts, Amherst, production of anthrax, again with some resisters going to jail
- advocated for providing shelter for the homeless more than thirty years ago in a Northampton Take-Off-The-Boards campaign
- with the American Friends Service Committee, counseled hundreds of young men to resist the draft, especially during the American-driven war in Vietnam
- organized voting campaigns
- encouraged investors, particularly colleges and universities, to stop supporting the South Africa apartheid government

My longtime association with Northampton's Claudia Lefko serves as one of my favorite experiences among many that resulted in enduring associations and friendships. I met Claudia in 1998 at a time when others and I planned our defense during our trial as the Raytheon Peacemakers who blocked the gate of the Andover defense contractor. As I handed out leaflets at the Northampton Recycling Center, I recognized Claudia and approached her to ask if she had considered acting to resist US sanctions against Iraq years before the US invaded Iraq.

Claudia traveled to our trial in Andover, where the former United States attorney general, Ramsey Clark, advised our resistance group during a high-profile trial that lasted several days. Unusually, Judge Ellen Flatley allowed us to employ the necessity defense to justify our actions at Raytheon: we said we had to block the gate to shut down the defense contractor in order to save others from injury and death. Nevertheless, the jury found us all guilty, and Judge Flatley assigned us to community service.

Claudia wrote about the trial and other resistance activities for the *Daily Hampshire Gazette*. A talented artist and teacher, she also established the Iraqi Children's Art Exchange. Claudia traveled periodically to Iraq to foster the exchange and bring aid to the Iraqi people. She found many opportunities to show the art of Iraqi children in the United States as she built a case for lifting US sanctions in Iraq.

Claudia also became instrumental in the work of the Northampton Committee to Lift the Sanctions, later the Northampton Committee to Stop Wars, referred to by its website, northamptoncommittee.org, as Northampton Committee to Stop the Wars. The Northampton Committee provided a natural transition for AFSC supporters and for me, and the committee often collaborated with AFSC. Northampton, the Valley, and other central Massachusetts and southern Vermont communities have a substantial core of dedicated workers for peace and justice, and together they pitch in to support endeavors aimed at righting wrongs perpetuated by government and corporate policies.

Just a few weeks ago, in a very personal effort that touched my heart, Claudia organized friends from past community actions of all kinds to celebrate my hundredth birthday with a hundred signs and a walk through Northampton. I am so grateful for the tribute.

Over the years, I have made countless friends in the course of community organizing efforts designed to bring social justice and peace to our world. May we someday see the elimination of war, discrimination, and repression. What a wonderful world that would be.

What Can We Do, Today, About Climate Change?
May 2019

As our climate warms because of our addiction to fossil fuels and more, we all pay a high price for the many conveniences available to us in 2019 USA.

Our infrastructure crumbles despite easy availability of gasoline for our automobiles. We demean the humanity of immigrants finding their way to our borders often because of our wars. Waging war costs not only in treasure and human lives, but also in constant release of carbon dioxide, the source of global warming. Ocean waters rise to threaten our coastlines, species become extinct, animals' migratory patterns shift, and still we indulge mindlessly in products and services that warm the planet.

As global warming threatens us all, heartless US policies defy common sense as our nation refuses to participate in sensible international efforts to reverse the effects of greenhouse gases. Global warming brings severe weather, says the National Resources Defense Council, along with dirty air and persistent threat to human health. NRDC says that fossil fuels, especially coal, create the most CO_2 at 2 billion tons annually, followed by transportation at 1.7 billion tons annually.

Losing Earth: A Climate History, a new book by Nathaniel Rich, explains that the oil industry operates at the heart of global warming. The author says we've created more CO_2 since 1989 than in all preceding generations.

Global warming first came to my attention in 1997 after my husband, Tom, died. I felt irresponsible driving alone from Northampton to Mount Toby Quaker Meeting in Leverett, so I looked for someone to rideshare. Carl Davies stepped forward. As we rode, he introduced me to global warming. From Carl, I learned about Richard Heinberg, a journalist who has written extensively about global warming and now serves as the senior fellow at the Post Carbon Institute.

Carl and I brought Richard to speak at Amherst and Smith colleges in the late 1990s, and Richard met with a small group who wanted to decide what to do. There began some local efforts to address global warming. For example, in the days before Massachusetts laws stated, "No person shall stand in a roadway for the purpose of soliciting a ride," we encouraged hitchhiking to minimize use of gasoline by driving cars.

Michael Klare, a Five Colleges professor, wrote the indispensable *Resource Wars* and *Blood and Oil: The Dangers and Consequences of America's Growing Petroleum Dependency.* Michael has often spoken about peak oil and the likelihood that we'll run out before we figure out how to maintain our many petroleum-dependent conveniences.

I would like to see more solarization in Massachusetts cities and towns, including downtown Amherst and Northampton. I very much appreciate the complaint of young people who think that we all should have done something to prevent global warming but, instead, will hand the problem off to them.

And don't be fooled into thinking that nuclear power will offset global warming. It's a ruse perpetrated by the nuclear industry whose mining and transportation depend on fossil fuels. Nothing portends more danger than nuclear power, and we have never found a place to store nuclear waste.

In 1971, I read *Diet for a Small Planet*, a bestseller by Frances Moore Lappé, the first major book to note the enviornmental impact of meat production as wasteful and a contributor to global food scarcity. She argued for practicing a vegetarian lifestyle out of concerns about production of animal-based products. I have been a vegetarian ever since.

People can grow food in household gardens, support local farmers markets and cooperatives, and dine in vegetarian restaurants to resist global warming.

I don't travel in airplanes and, even when I had a car, I walked to errands. I brought a rolling cart to the grocery store.

We should have more free bus service and more public transportation.

People can always reuse and recycle. I love the slogan "Wear it out, use it up. If in doubt, do without." I endorse banning plastic bags, whose manufacture depends on fossil fuels. I shop for clothing in a used clothing store.

We have to turn things around, and we have to do it soon.

In It Together
June 2019

"How do you live so long?" people often ask me. I celebrated my hundredth birthday in March, and I see clear reasons for my longevity.

I grew up in Carthage, Missouri, a town with no polluting industries. My sisters and I received regular medical and dental attention. From an early age, I enjoyed physical activity, and I've made a practice of regular exercise all my life, including walking and swimming when more strenuous exercise evaded me as I aged.

Luckily, I've been able to maintain a solid mental life by reading and through purposeful activity especially aimed at ending war, abolishing nuclear weapons and nuclear power, living lightly on the earth, and encouraging local, national, and international peace without weapons.

For decades, since reading *Diet for a Small Planet* by Frances Moore Lappé in 1971, I've been a vegetarian.

I think it's important, as much as possible, to eat food produced locally. My friend Carolyn Oates Rosewarne, a Valley farmer and local food advocate, works with me together with other friends on my Northampton front-yard garden. For many reasons, Carolyn decided some years ago that she wanted to know where her food originates.

"Concerned for my own health and nutrition, the health of others, and the health of our planet," Carolyn told me, "I studied and learned about the food and healthcare industries. I wanted to know where my food comes from, how it's grown, how it's produced, and how animals are raised, fed, treated, and slaughtered."

Carolyn said her reading showed her the unhealthiness of mass-production food sources and systems that contribute to diseases and food allergies. Carolyn thinks that industrial food systems have resulted in sick people, animals, soils, air, and water contributing to human food allergies, especially because of the use of pesticides, antibiotics, and hormones. Carolyn wondered how we can change food production for the better.

"We make a choice every day with our food dollars," Carolyn told me. "We can choose to buy and eat food grown organically, sustainably, and humanely. We can educate ourselves to appreciate healthy alternatives to industrialized food. If we buy local food, we get to know farmers and grocers. When we grow and share food, we can create a better food system within our communities."

Each week for many years, Carolyn has made me soups using fresh, local, and in-season vegetables. Not only do I enjoy delicious soup, but I know that when we eat food produced locally, we do not contribute to greenhouse gases produced during food transit. We don't contribute to food waste occurring during warehousing and transit. Instead, we contribute to the local economy and support local farmers.

Farm stands, farmers markets, mobile markets, community-supported agriculture, and food coops offer fresh fruits and vegetables along with locally produced cheese, meat, and eggs. Even in winter, farmers grow fresh produce in greenhouses, so all year round we can find fresh, locally grown food.

In order to build soil in my own garden, I keep a two-quart compost bucket next to my kitchen sink and place all food waste in it. Then, I see that the contents go to a compost bin in my back yard. After some months in the compost bin, ideally after someone layers it with ashes or leaves and turns it, the compost transforms—magically, it seems—into rich, fertile soil I can use in my front-yard garden.

Some people keep egg-laying birds, and many farm stands offer fresh eggs from their free-roaming hens, ducks, or even geese. Those eggs come from animals raised humanely, thus making their eggs a better choice.

Carolyn reminded me that recipients of federal Supplementary Nutrition Assistance Program (SNAP) benefits may take advantage of state Healthy Incentives Program (HIP) benefits during some months in order to buy more fruits and vegetables, including in shares of community supported agriculture, CSA, from approved retailers.

All year round in the Pioneer Valley, we can all take advantage of the abundance of local food for healthier families and a healthier planet.

I Couldn't Imagine No *Democracy Now!*
July 2019

Like many people in the Valley and across the country, I couldn't imagine a weekday without Amy Goodman's news program, *Democracy Now!* Amy and her colleagues invite influential people to speak for themselves about events without the filters of mainstream news practices. And Amy and her colleagues often realize that mainstream news outlets do not necessarily recognize nor include many of the most important influencers.

Think Medea Benjamin or the Berrigans or Allan Nairn or Noam Chomsky or John Bonifaz or Sut Jhally, among many others, who challenge conventional United States expectations by speaking truth to power or revealing information that mainstream outlets might suppress. Amy and her cohosts interview them and others to illuminate our understanding of our nation and our world.

I think *Democracy Now!* is a superb, reliable program available at eight each weekday morning on Northampton Cable Television, NCTV, Channel 12, and on WMUA radio. Valley Free Radio, WXOJ, broadcasts *Democracy Now!* daily at five each afternoon. It also airs whenever anyone wants at democracynow.org.

Even though I look forward to beginning the day with *Democracy Now!* it wasn't always easy. *Democracy Now!* began broadcasting from New York in 1996, but we didn't have it nor

*During celebrations for Frances's one-hundredth birthday,
Amy Goodman interviews Frances at Smith College.*

any other alternative independent media in the Valley until
after September 11, 2001.

I had heard about *Democracy Now!* before a trip to my
family in Maine soon after 9/11, but I hadn't heard the
program till I was there listening every day to Maine Public
Radio. Hearing Amy and her show convinced me that I wanted
to bring *Democracy Now!* to the Valley.

When I returned from Maine, I approached local public
radio with the idea that *Democracy Now!* would appeal to
Valley audiences. However, radio station management
disagreed, and no one in authority supported the idea.

Then the late Ed Russell took the initiative to see me one
day at our Northampton Vigil to Stop the Wars. I learned that
Ed, a local musician and activist, downloaded the program to a
compact disc every day, then climbed Mount Holyoke in order
to find a radio signal he could use to broadcast *Democracy Now!*
to those who could pick up Ed's signal.

Around the same time, organizers at Judson Memorial Church in Washington Square, Greenwich Village, invited me to participate in an event where, serendipitously, I met Amy Goodman. We spoke at length, and I became more convinced than ever that the Valley needed wide access to *Democracy Now!* I went to the top of Mount Holyoke to discuss the possibility with Ed Russell.

Little did I know at the time that I would eventually become good friends with Claudia Lefko, who sometimes helped her friend Ed Russell with the broadcasts.

Ed and I decided that I would put a radio tower in my back yard in order to broadcast *Democracy Now!* At first, he thought maybe a church steeple would be best, but because of a disability that made it very difficult for him to walk, we decided on my backyard instead.

As soon as the tower went up, he set up a broadcast and drove around Northampton in his car to see if he could hear the program on the frequency 92.3. Yes, he could. He continued to help us with the broadcast

For many years, we broadcast *Democracy Now!* on my backyard tower until local stations eventually picked up the broadcast.

Sadly, Ed Russell died this year almost at the same time as celebrations Claudia organized in honor of my hundredth birthday. His friends plan a memorial for him sometime this summer. Valley Free Radio will accept donations in his name. Ed would have loved to hear Amy Goodman at Smith College when she came to speak there in March.

As for me, I'm glad for Amy's friendship, and I am endlessly grateful for Ed Russell's determination in bringing *Democracy Now!* to our area. It just shows what can happen when a community joins together in the name of conscience and truth. *Democracy Now!* has provided the surrounding community with ways to think differently about war and peace.

Nuclear Freeze
August 2019

So many lives changed on August 6, 1945, including mine. I was a twenty-year-old American married to an aspiring radiologist. I listened to the radio as I ironed our clothes and learned that my country, the United States, had destroyed Hiroshima, Japan, by dropping an atomic bomb on it.

Perhaps, seventy-four years later, we're immune to the consequences of what happened that day and on August 9, 1945, when we dropped another atomic bomb on Nagasaki, Japan.

The United States is the only nation in the world to have destroyed whole cities by dropping atomic bombs. We have also used radioactive depleted uranium on battlefields in Iraq, according to US Defense Department records, and who knows where else.

Our economy depends on the fact that the United States spends more on its military budget than any nation in the world: $649 billion, more than double the military budget of China at $250 billion, next in line.

Make no mistake. Donald Trump's flashy July 4 celebration of war and weapons in Washington, DC, calculated around selling US weapons to whomever in the world: ironically, Japan and, oh, say, Saudi Arabia, Russia, China itself, Brazil, Mexico, and who knows who else?

Today, according to the Federation of American Scientists, the US has nearly four thousand nuclear weapons stockpiled, much more deadly than what we dropped on Hiroshima and Nagasaki in 1945.

Only the United States has ever waged nuclear war.

A study by Ira Helfand of the International Physicians for the Prevention of Nuclear War states that 100 Hiroshima-sized bombs could endanger the lives of 2 billion people on this planet. Most of the weapons in the United States arsenal are many times more powerful than that.

In 1980, though, we had nearly thirty thousand nuclear bombs in our arsenal. I worried about what that meant for the world and launched a western Massachusetts campaign to freeze the development of nuclear weapons. That campaign eventually became national as people mobilized all over Massachusetts and the country to enact a freeze on nuclear weapons.

In the early 1980s, I found out about Dr. Randall Forsberg's *Call to Halt the Arms Race*, the manifesto of the nuclear freeze campaign. Dr. Forsberg was associated with the Massachusetts Institute of Technology and had access to credible statistics about why to halt US manufacture of nuclear weapons.

Make no mistake. A relatively small amount of nuclear weapons can cause devastation to the world's population. Perhaps no concern — not even global warming — rings more imminent than worrying about nuclear weapons.

When I heard about Randy Forsberg's initiative in the early 1980s, I went to the national American Friends Service Committee and proposed western Massachusetts involvement in a campaign for a freeze on US manufacture of nuclear weapons.

The Friends said, "Yes, Frances. Please do mount a campaign to freeze US manufacture of nuclear weapons." I collaborated with Randy Kehler, then executive director of the Traprock Peace Center in Deerfield. We hired Judith Scheckel to coordinate our western Massachusetts nuclear freeze campaign by placing it on a referendum in congressional districts.

People mobilized by going door-to-door to get out the vote to support the nuclear freeze. Today, people would launch a big social media campaign, but in the 1980s, we didn't have social media. Ronald Reagan, the Republican candidate, got lots of votes, but so did the freeze as a result of our mobilization.

In 1982, voters in eight states and several major cities, including one-fourth of the country's population, voted for a worldwide nuclear freeze. In Massachusetts, nearly three-quarters—73.7 percent—voted in favor.

Because of the 1980s freeze campaign, the United States reduced its stockpile of nuclear weapons and created a model for mobilization. But we still have about 4,000 nuclear weapons in our military stockpile. It's time to mobilize again to get rid of them.

In order to sell weapons, including nuclear, to nations all over the world, President Trump staged a huge display of weaponry on the Washington Mall on Independence Day.

But nuclear weapons aren't playthings even though they underpin the U.S's policy of war, which serves as part of the basis of the US economy. We should never forget that it doesn't take many of them to destroy the world.

Now is the time to make a difference. Now is the time to stop building nuclear weapons.

Resisting Nuclear Submarines
September 2019

For many years, many of us waged a vigorous campaign to halt construction of Trident nuclear submarines, each bearing forty weapons that include a number of Trident nuclear missiles capable of destroying areas the size of several countries or even a continent.

In the 1980s, with the help of my Northampton friends Sally Mazloski and Meg Gage, I managed to make my way through a big crowd gathered for the launch of a Trident at the General Dynamics Electric Boat facility in Groton, Connecticut.

I had a baby bottle of my own blood to signify the destructive capability of the submarine and its missiles. I managed to pour my blood on the submarine before it launched.

The crowd surrounded me as people tore at my clothes, scratched my face and arms, and pulled my hair. I was never so relieved as when the police came to arrest me. Although the state dropped charges against me, on another occasion at Electric Boat, I ended up serving thirty days in York Correctional Institution in Niantic, Connecticut.

It was all worth it. We have to stop making nuclear weapons of all kinds. We have more than four thousand nuclear weapons in the United States arsenal today. We have to stop the madness.

The United States Navy sponsors Trident submarines. Most recently, at the launch of the USS *Vermont* at Electric Boat on

October 20, 2018, Vermont's US Democratic Congressman, Representative Peter Welch, said the vessel is vitally important to the strategic defense of the US, according to *US Navy Times*.

"The United States is the biggest dealer in death in the world," counters my friend Hattie Nestel, who once interrupted the launch speech of William Cohen, then secretary of defense, at a US Aegis cruiser launch. I agree with Hattie and not with Representative Welch.

Our military budget grows and grows and grows. How many times over do we have to have the capability of destroying the world?

When a nuclear submarine or other United States Navy war vessel launches, the government throws a big party with invited public and military officials. A woman has cracked a bottle of champagne on the prow of the submarine in order to signify its naming. Until 1997, she was identified in terms of her husband's name, as in Mrs. Dwight D. Eisenhower. At least now she is identified with her own name and title, as in Dr. Jill Biden, who broke the bottle over the USS *Delaware* the same day as Gloria Valdez, former deputy US secretary of the navy, broke a bottle of Putney Mountain Winery sparkling wine over the USS *Vermont*.

The Lockheed Martin Corporation of Sunnyvale, California, designs the D5 nuclear ballistic missiles carried by nuclear submarines. Each Virginia Class submarine like the *Vermont* or *Delaware* sets taxpayers back 2.8 billion dollars.

Groton's Electric Boat facility has nine more such submarines in the pipeline.

With the Atlantic Life Community founded by Philip Berrigan and Elizabeth McAlister, I participated in many demonstrations against Trident launches during the 1980s and 1990s. Despite arms limitation treaties and nuclear freezes, the US Navy constantly updates our submarine arsenal with advanced nuclear submarines and missiles.

Defense contractors like General Dynamics and Lockheed Martin prosper with the buildup while the government cages immigrant children at the US border, imprisons more individuals per capita than any nation in the world, and withholds health care from the poorest among us. General Dynamics expects to employ thirteen thousand people by 2034 at Electric Boat to manufacture nuclear ballistic missile submarines, according to its website.

It devastated me when the US dropped the first atomic bombs in 1945 on Hiroshima and Nagasaki. I had no idea how diabolically our nation would nurture its investment in death and destruction as we have, indeed, become the biggest dealer in death in the world.

We surely could put our talents to better use.

Learning That War Is Not the Answer
October 2019
• previously not published •
**written for October, 2019 publication in the *Daily Hampshire Gazette*
but not submitted after Frances's August 27, 2019 death**

Throughout my life, I've strived to follow my conscience
and encourage others to find their right truths and follow
them. To do so, I've developed my abilities to interact
positively with people.

Growing up in Carthage, Missouri, provided a great
backdrop for discerning common ground and working well
with others. However, during my young adulthood in New
York City as World War II raged in Europe and Asia, I found
work in the defense industry that helped me develop my
people skills—and eventually led me to realize that war is not
the answer.

When my physician husband, Tom, decided to go into
the army after the bombing of Pearl Harbor in 1941, I tried to
think of a way to get involved.

The whole ethos of the time was commitment to the war.

I thought about women's military groups or the American
Red Cross, but none appealed to me.

Then I went to a Mount Holyoke program with an entrée
into wartime industries for graduates looking for a job. As
thousands of men joined the armed forces, manufacturing
companies wanted to train women to work in factories geared
up to build the implements of war. I learned firsthand about

the defense industry. The course emphasized personnel administration and other skills.

I got a job right away at Sperry Gyroscope on Long Island.

I decided to live in Manhattan, where I found a room at International House near Columbia University where I planned to do graduate work in psychology.

Unfortunately, at Sperry everything seemed disorganized. After a while, I decided to change jobs. I looked around and got a job at Bell Telephone Laboratories in Greenwich Village. A well established firm, Bell developed communications systems for the war. It had a women's division with its own personnel department with women in charge, and that's where I worked. I found it refreshing to work with women.

It's interesting how you do things at a given time without considering the implications. In hindsight, I realize that the corporate war culture had grabbed my mind.

I got to Bell Labs by a much easier commute than I had going to Sperry. At a station not far from International House, I got on the A Train, the Seventh Avenue subway. I got off at Twelfth Street and walked a few short blocks to work. It often took less than half an hour instead of the previous hour and a half I spent going to Long Island.

With my job at Bell Labs, I could more easily do graduate work. After working full time six days a week, I took classes at Columbia at night.

I wanted to understand more about why we were at war, though, and the courses I took at Columbia didn't serve. I heard about the New School for Social Research offering courses on world politics, and I decided to leave Columbia. The New School was close to my work. From 1934, its University in Exile provided refuge for scholars fleeing anti-Semitic persecution in Germany. Refugees from Russia and Germany brought fresh perspective, and I took their courses for insight into circumstances surrounding the war in Europe.

New York not only provided challenging ideas. I found opportunities to keep up with the physical activity I loved. At the New Dance Group in Greenwich Village, I took a dance class with Pearl Primus, a talented interpreter of African dance.

Living at International House and working in New York exposed me to ideas and perspectives I had not encountered in Missouri or Syracuse. I learned about the suffering of war victims and inequities causing war and resulting from it. By the end of my three-and-a-half-year stay in New York, I was ready to say, "War is not the answer."

I also learned how to interact with people in ways that would serve my conscience well as I counseled draft resisters and worked with peace groups throughout my career.

Surrounded by family, Frances died during the morning of August 27, 2019.

DESIDERATA

GO PLACIDLY amid the noise and the haste, and remember what peace there may be in silence. As far as possible, without surrender, be on good terms with all persons.

Speak your truth quietly and clearly; and listen to others, even to the dull and the ignorant; they too have their story.

Avoid loud and aggressive persons; they are vexatious to the spirit. If you compare yourself with others, you may become vain or bitter, for always there will be greater and lesser persons than yourself.

Enjoy your achievements as well as your plans. Keep interested in your own career, however humble; it is a real possession in the changing fortunes of time.

Exercise caution in your business affairs, for the world is full of trickery. But let this not blind you to what virtue there is; many persons strive for high ideals, and everywhere life is full of heroism.

Be yourself. Especially do not feign affection. Neither be cynical about love; for in the face of all aridity and disenchantment, it is as perennial as the grass.

Take kindly the counsel of the years, gracefully surrendering the things of youth.

Nurture strength of spirit to shield you in sudden misfortune. But do not distress yourself with dark imaginings. Many fears are born of fatigue and loneliness.

Beyond a wholesome discipline, be gentle with yourself. You are a child of the universe no less than the trees and the stars; you have a right to be here.

And whether or not it is clear to you, no doubt the universe is unfolding as it should. Therefore be at peace with God, whatever you conceive Him to be. And whatever your labors and aspirations, in the noisy confusion of life, keep peace in your soul. With all its sham, drudgery and broken dreams, it is still a beautiful world. Be cheerful. Strive to be happy.

—Max Ehrmann © 1927

*Frances's extensive collection of peace buttons decorate
an Asian robe with Vietnamese farmer's hat,*

Frances's light shines on.

CPSIA information can be obtained
at www.ICGtesting.com
Printed in the USA
FSHW020724170920
73265FS

9 781948 380317